# CONTENTS

Words that appear in the text in bold, **like this**, are explained in the glossary.

N
W E
S

Vienna

Constantinople
(Istanbul)

SPAIN
Granada
Cordoba
Rome

SICILY

ATLANTIC
OCEAN
TUNISIA
MEDITERRANEA

MOROCCO
Cairo
EGYPT

AFRICA

SONGHAI
Dome of the Rock

MALI

Area ruled by the Islamic Empires by 750

Area ruled by the Islamic Empires by 1250

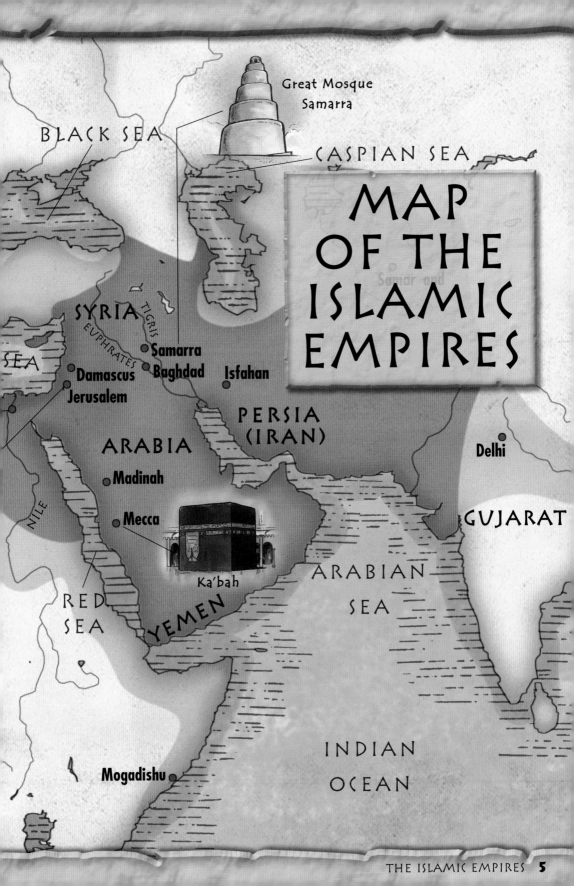

Great Mosque
Samarra

BLACK SEA

CASPIAN SEA

# MAP OF THE ISLAMIC EMPIRES

SYRIA

TIGRIS

EUPHRATES

SEA

Samarra
Damascus Baghdad
Jerusalem

Isfahan

PERSIA
(IRAN)

ARABIA

Delhi

Madinah

NILE

Mecca

GUJARAT

Ka'bah

ARABIAN

SEA

RED
SEA

YEMEN

INDIAN

OCEAN

Mogadishu

This is the Dome of the Rock, a beautiful and important Muslim mosque in Jerusalem.

# CHAPTER 1

# FACTS ABOUT THE ISLAMIC EMPIRES

Welcome to one of the most fascinating civilizations in history, the Islamic Empires. There's a lot to take in because the empires cover such a large portion of the continent of Asia, as well as parts of Africa and Europe. They also span a very long period in history. This section tells you all you need to know about the best and worst times to visit, and what the climate and different landscapes are like. It also gives you some important background information about the Muslim way of life and who's who in this vast, exciting world.

# WHEN TO VISIT

You will have to get your timing right to see the glories of the Islamic Empires. There was no Islamic world to visit before around AD 620. This was when the words of **Allah** (God) were first revealed to the **Prophet Muhammad** and the religion of **Islam** began in **Mecca**, in present-day Saudi Arabia. After this, many people **converted** to Islam. Some converts changed to Islam because they thought it was a simpler and better religion. Some were persuaded to become **Muslims** because it often meant paying lower taxes and the chance of better schooling and jobs.

Some people were forced to convert to the Islamic religion, when Muslim armies attacked and took control of the regions in which they lived.

## EXPANSION

The Islamic world expanded steadily during Muhammad's life and continued to increase in size after the Prophet's death in AD 632. At this time the Islamic world was ruled by religious leaders called **caliphs**. By AD 640 it included what is now Syria, Egypt, Iraq, and Israel. The first major Islamic Empire, called the **Umayyad** Empire, started in AD 661. The Umayyad Empire expanded rapidly. By AD 711, its caliphs controlled land stretching from western Spain to Afghanistan in the East.

## GOLDEN AGE

The best time to visit the Islamic Empires is between AD 750 and 1258. This period is often known as the Golden Age of Islam. During this period the caliphs' interest in science and knowledge encouraged the spread of new ideas and inventions all over their lands.

## PEACEFUL CONQUEST

The Islamic Empires were unusually merciful towards people in conquered territories compared with many other empires. For example, Khalid ibn al-Walid, a 7th-century Muslim general, offered the people of Damascus:

" . . . security for their lives, prosperity and churches. Their city walls shall not be demolished, neither shall any Muslim be quartered in their houses. Thereunto we give them the pact of Allah and the protection of his Prophet, the caliphs and the believers. So long as they pay the poll tax, nothing but good shall befall them."

## GOOD AND BAD TIMES TO VISIT

| | |
|---|---|
| AD 610 | The Prophet Muhammad turns to the religion of Islam after the Angel Jibril (Gabriel) reveals Allah's truth to him. |
| 622 | Muhammad and his followers are chased out of Mecca. |
| 632 | Prophet Muhammad dies. |
| 661 | Umayyad Empire begins. |
| 750 | **Abbasid** Empire begins. |
| 762 | Baghdad becomes capital of the Islamic Empires. |
| 750–1258 | Era often known as the Golden Age. |
| 800–900 | Muhammad's sayings and teachings, called Hadiths, collected together. |
| 836 | Capital of Islamic Empires moves to Samarra, following unrest in Baghdad. |
| 892 | Capital returns to Baghdad. |
| 1095–1291 | The **Crusades**: Muslims and Christians fight for control of many previously Muslim regions. |
| 1258 | **Mongols** attack Baghdad, and Abbasid rule comes to an end. |

Key:

Stay away        Interesting times to visit        Best times to visit

# LANDSCAPE AND CLIMATE

During the Golden Age the Islamic Empires stretch across many different landscapes, from warm coasts to high, cold mountains. However, most of the empires' lands are in western Asia and North Africa with a hot, dry, desert climate. It hardly rains here and you'll find deserts full of shifting sand dunes and barren rocks. Because there is little water, very few plants grow, so there is hardly any shade from the burning sun during the day. Few people live in one place in the desert. Most pass through, resting at scattered **oases**, or water holes, but these are few and far between. If you don't know where you're going, you could risk dying of thirst.

## PACK SOMETHING WARM

Travellers to the desert often make the mistake of packing only hot weather gear. But, because there are no plants to trap the heat at ground level and because dry air cools quickly, a desert can become freezing cold at night. Locals wear animal furs to keep warm but you may prefer to pack a thick coat. The Sahara in North Africa (below) is the largest desert in the world. Winds here can blow for days at a time, blasting sand and dust into your eyes and face.

## RIVERS, MARSHES, AND MOUNTAINS

Many settlements in the Islamic Empires are near permanent water sources. For example, the capital city of the Abbasid Empire, Baghdad, is at the meeting point of two major rivers, the Tigris and Euphrates. And the biggest city of the **Fatimid** Empire, Cairo, is on the mighty River Nile. Around the rivers there are fields of crops and groves of date palms and orange trees. Fishermen cast nets from the shore and trading boats busily sail the waters.

While you're visiting the Islamic Empires, it's also worth going to the vast marshy area south of Baghdad. The Marsh Arabs who live here cut down the abundant reeds growing in the mud and weave them together to make floating villages. See if you can look inside one of their enormous *mudhifs* (village meeting rooms). If you get really sick of the heat you can climb a mountain in Turkey or Iraq to cool off.

# ISLAMIC RELIGION

Wherever you go in the Islamic Empires you will be aware of the influence of Islam. Religion affects almost every part of a good Muslim person's life so it is useful to know something about the background to Islam before you go.

Muslims believe that the Angel Jibril (Gabriel) came to Earth and passed on a series of **revelations** from Allah (God) to the Prophet Muhammad. When the Prophet first told people about this he gained enemies, and he and his followers were forced out of Mecca to **Madinah** in the north. But gradually Muhammad persuaded others of the truth of Islam. After Muhammad's death in AD 632, the revelations were remembered and eventually recorded in the **Qur'an**, the Muslim holy book.

## PRAYER RITUAL

Muslims are reminded that it is time to pray at the **mosque** by the **muezzin**. He calls out the **Shahadah** from the high tower (minaret) on the mosque. Inside, the **imam** leads the prayers and all worshippers face in the direction of Mecca.

## THE FIVE PILLARS

The Five Pillars are things any good Muslim should believe or do in his or her life. Knowing what these are will give you an insight into some of the aspects of Muslim life you'll encounter on your trip.

1. Shahadah is saying that you believe in Islam. You will see or hear variations of the phrase "There is no God but Allah and Muhammad is the Messenger of Allah" everywhere you go.

2. One thing you are sure to notice is that the streets are empty of men at midday on Friday. That's because this is a time for prayer for all Muslim males. All Muslims, male and female, pray five times each day, but not always at the mosque.

3. The third pillar is charity and you'll often see Muslims giving money (up to a tenth of their income) to the needy.

4. At **Ramadan** Muslims do not eat or drink for a month during the hours of daylight to recall the time the Prophet received the revelations.

5. All Muslims try to make a hajj (**pilgrimage**) to the holy city of Mecca once in their lifetime. Mecca is holy because it is where the Prophet received the revelations.

If you are not a Muslim, you don't need to follow the five pillars and you will still be welcome in the Islamic Empires. The Qur'an teaches that Muslims should be tolerant of people of other religions and places. In the Islamic Empires some people of other religions have high social status.

At Mecca, Muslim pilgrims circle a sacred structure called the Ka'bah. This contains a holy black stone that Muslims believe was sent from Heaven to Earth by Allah. ↘

# WHO'S WHO IN THE ISLAMIC WORLD?

As a visitor, you need to understand the different levels of society in the Islamic Empires. The most important people are the caliphs and **sultans**. Sultans are kings who rule particular areas, and everyone has to treat them with great respect. They live in luxurious homes and surround themselves with trusted bodyguards, tutors, and advisers. Next in line are the **amirs** (military leaders) and then the government officials, such as tax collectors and lawyers.

Merchants and traders are also quite well to do, and live in very comfortable houses. The majority of ordinary men in the Islamic Empires work as farmers. The lowest-ranking people are those who do lowly or dirty jobs. Below them are slaves who have been captured from foreign lands.

## FAMILY LIFE

Family connections are really important in the Islamic Empires. Different branches of the same family usually live near each other, and several generations often share the same home. Sons and their families generally live with and care for their parents. Daughters often marry second or third cousins and move away. Uncles or cousins often train older boys to do the same jobs as them, so it's common to have whole families of blacksmiths or soldiers, for instance.

### SPECIAL SLAVES

Mamluks are special slaves who are educated and trained to be private soldiers and advisers for caliphs and sultans. These slaves have been captured and brought from far distant areas, to make sure they have no family links with enemies of the empires. Some mamluks with extraordinary skills became very powerful rulers themselves. For example, Salah ad-Din, the military leader of the Islamic armies in the 11th century, was once a mamluk.

# WOMEN AND CHILDREN

What you can do and where you can go in the Islamic Empires depends to a large extent on whether you are male or female. Depending on the family's economic situation, most women spend their days doing household chores or supervising the servants, taking care of children, praying, sewing and doing embroidery, weaving, or playing music. Most girls don't go to school. They learn how to run the home and fetch water from the well or river, or search for fuel for the fire.

Boys might look after herds of animals or work in the fields. Some young boys go to the **madrassah** to learn about their religion. Young boys and girls might play games together, but as they get older, girls stay at home more to keep out of sight of men. This shows that they respect Islamic life. Most girls marry very young – aged 12 or 13.

This family of pilgrims have stopped in the desert, on their way to Mecca. The mother and child can be seen in the tent. ⌐↪

Camels are the only reliable means of transport across the vast and lonely desert.

# CHAPTER 2

# ON THE MOVE

Before you set off on your adventures there are some bits of practical information you need to know. You can get into real trouble if you wear the wrong clothes or make the wrong gestures. When you're on the move you may be covering some seriously long distances, so you'll need to know the ups and downs of camel travel! Being a tourist in the Islamic Empires can also be hazardous: many die along the way from thirst, hunger, or overexposure to the Sun.

# GETTING AROUND

As a tourist in the Islamic world you'll never get lonely as people are always on the move. Students and scholars travel to Baghdad and other major cities in order to study under great masters. Large armies are constantly on their way to conquer new lands, and **nomads** travel from place to place. And then there are all the pilgrims travelling to and from Mecca.

## BY LAND

Many people ride horses or donkeys in the Islamic Empires, but camels are the only animals that can travel long distances across barren land without needing water. Huge camel **caravans**, with lines of up to 2,000 camels, travel across the empires, trading in goods such as gold and salt. Ask the locals where the best camel markets are and always hire a guide to travel with you – it's easy to get lost in a desert!

## BY SEA

For some journeys you'll need to hitch a ride on one of the Muslim trading ships. You'll find these **dhows** at new city ports such as Basrah. Dhows carry a crew of 30 or more, so you could work on board to pay for your passage.

This 12th-century map shows the Red Sea and the towns of Madinah (top) and Mecca (bottom). It may look simple but maps of the Islamic Empires were the best in the world for their time.

They use their vast triangular sails to catch seasonal **monsoon** winds that take them to faraway ports during winter, and bring them back in the summer. But sea travel is only for the brave. Ships are made of wooden planks that can be wrecked by storms. And even though Muslims control the seas, there are many pirates waiting to rob and kill those on board.

## TRAVEL AIDS

The **astrolabe** is a new invention that you can use to read the positions of the stars and planets to help you navigate. And if you visit after the 14th century Muslim travellers also use the compass, adopted from the Chinese, to help them find their way around.

## TRAVELLER'S TIPS

- Bring some snacks! Most travellers eat dried fruits and nuts or olives.
- Bring along a soft cushion for a camel trip. As camels walk, their bodies rock and bump from side to side, so you should probably prepare for some travel sickness.
- Camel travel is slow — you'll only cover a maximum of about 40 kilometres (25 miles) per day. But a big advantage is that you can use dried camel dung to make camp fires to warm you up on cold desert nights!
- It's also a good idea to buy some sweet-smelling frankincense or myrrh to rub under your nose before you set off. They are expensive but worth it — camels are famous for their bad breath!

# WHERE TO STAY

Muslims have a tradition of hospitality and charity. They are very welcoming to pilgrims and travellers, so it should be quite easy for you to find places to stay while travelling through the empires.

## IN TOWNS AND CITIES

When you visit towns and cities you'll probably be offered a bed for free in a private home. You might also be able to stay in one of the dormitories that you often find attached to a mosque. These are intended to provide bed and breakfast for weary Muslim pilgrims.

Homes in the Islamic Empires obviously vary in size and style, depending on the wealth of the owner and on where you are in the empires. But a typical Muslim home will be rectangular, with an open courtyard in the middle and surrounded by high walls. Inside there are usually colourful rugs covering the floor and low couches with cushions you can lounge on.

## OUT OF BOUNDS

Homes are separated into men's and women's sections. The women's section is called the **harem** and is usually at the back and is out of bounds for men. If you wander into the wrong part you could get yourself into some serious trouble!

The centre of this caravanserai courtyard in Turkey has a small oratory, a place where travellers can pray.

## IN THE COUNTRYSIDE

Outside the towns and cities, you should look for one of the many **caravanserais** that are scattered across the barren parts of the empires. Rulers ordered these roadside inns to be built to encourage trade. They are about one day's caravan travel apart. They allow caravans to stay one or two nights to rest and recover before continuing their journey. Every caravanserai has a large courtyard where you can leave your camels, horses, or donkeys and where they are given water and food. There are also storage rooms where traders can leave their goods, and bedrooms for the travellers. Muslim travellers can take the chance to pray in a caravanserai, and everyone should take a bath – unless they want to become as smelly as the camels!

In a caravanserai you'll get a chance to put your feet up and share travel tips with other tourists, traders, or pilgrims, while the animals rest.

# WHAT TO WEAR

Even though it's hot in most parts of the Islamic Empires, don't pack your shorts and T-shirts. That would be a sure-fire way to cause great offence and get into big trouble. People in most parts of the Islamic Empires believe that Allah wants people, especially women, to be modest. All women are expected to cover themselves thoroughly when they are in public, so that men who are not their husbands cannot look at their bodies.

## WOMEN'S WEAR

Girls and women should wear a long, loose robe that covers their ankles. Alternatively they should wear a loose tunic that goes below the knees and a pair of baggy trousers to go underneath this. Make sure you get them made of cotton or linen because these fabrics are cool and good at absorbing sweat. Don't forget to buy a matching veil as well. To fit in, you'll need to pull the veil across your face when you're out and about, but you can loosen it again when you're inside.

This woman's costume is typical of the clothes worn by girls and women in the Islamic Empires.

### BE SAFE IN THE SUN

Sun cream is not available yet, so wearing long loose clothes is the only way to prevent sunburn. Wear white or light-coloured robes because these reflect (rather than absorb) the heat and will help to keep you cool. In the desert wear a scarf around your head, like the locals, to stop sand blowing into your eyes and mouth.

## MEN'S FASHION TIPS

Men should wear long loose shirts and baggy trousers too, but get your tunic hemmed carefully because Muslims in the empires believed you would end up in hell if your tunic was too long. They also wear a long piece of cloth as a sort of cloak. This can double as both a sunshade and an umbrella, depending on the weather. In some places, men wear a turban, a long piece of cloth wound tightly around the head that also protects them from the desert sand and sun. Many Arab men are proud of their turbans and it is considered a great insult to knock off another man's turban!

Finally, the Qur'an tells men they should not wear silk clothes or gold jewellery. If you do, people will think you're a big show-off who is bragging about his wealth and you won't be welcome anywhere.

This man is wearing the long tunic and turban favoured by most men during the Golden Age of the Islamic Empires.

# FOOD AND DRINK

The food you'll be offered in the Islamic Empires will vary from place to place, but generally it will be healthy and delicious. There are figs and oranges, olives, dishes made with aubergines, and flat breads and grains. Sheep's milk and goat's milk are used to make yoghurt and feta cheese. Pudding lovers can get sweet pastries made with sugar, honey, nuts, eggs, and dried fruit. Spicy foods are made using flavourings such as cinnamon, cumin, and cloves, which are bought and sold by traders. But watch out because there are no fridges, and spices often disguise the taste of food that has gone off!

## FEAST OR FAMINE?

You should find plenty to eat on your travels. Muslim farmers use dung and other fertilizers to help grow healthy crops. They also build canals and water wheels to channel or collect water to **irrigate** their dry lands. But you'll go hungry if you arrive in an area that has just been hit by a plague of locusts. A swarm of these grasshopper-like insects can destroy a field of grain in hours, a fact that earns them a mention in the Qur'an.

Many markets in the Islamic Empires have colourful, strong-smelling spices for sale. Just follow your nose and you'll find them!

## MEATY MEALS

For those of you who can't last a week without ham or bacon, here is the bad news. The eating of pork is forbidden, partly because pigs are considered unclean animals. But you can eat meat from other animals as long as it is **halal**, which means the animals have been slaughtered humanely. Islamic law says that people should be kind to all Allah's creatures, so animals have their throats slit to cause them minimum suffering. Camel and goat meat are two local delicacies you might like to try.

Here, cooks knead bread and stir bubbling cauldrons of meat over open fires in preparation for a large meal.

### ELEPHANT MEAT

Muslims are also discouraged from eating elephant meat. If you ask why, you may get to hear an old legend about a **sheikh** and 30 men who got lost on a mountain. Even though the sheikh told them not to, the hungry men killed and ate a small elephant. That night elephants killed all the men, but carried the sheikh safely back to a village.

## DRINKS

You won't go thirsty in the cities. To fulfil their promise to donate to charity (the fourth Pillar of Islam), wealthy Muslims build public drinking fountains where everyone can get fresh drinking water. And when you arrive at someone's house the first thing they'll do is offer you a drink – perhaps a sweet mint tea or even juice made from sugary lemon syrup.

# CUSTOMS AND BELIEFS

Some of the most important Muslim customs are connected with mosques. At the door, all worshippers must take off their shoes and wash in a fountain or pool there. This ritual washing is called *wudu* and it symbolizes people wanting to make themselves pure and clean before worshipping Allah.

Inside, all the male worshippers sit on the floor as a sign that they are all considered equal by Allah. When women come to the mosque they always have their heads covered and sit in a different part, but often they will pray at home instead.

Modern Muslims wash before entering a mosque, just as Muslims have always done.

⬅

## MARRIAGE CUSTOMS

The Islamic world at this time is not the place to look for a holiday romance. It is not the custom for young people to go on dates, because marriages are arranged by parents. The bride and groom often don't meet until their wedding day. Try to go to a Muslim wedding if you get the chance. The bride usually travels to the groom's house in a closed tent on a camel's back.

She is accompanied by musicians and men carrying gifts and her **dowry** (money from her family). The wedding celebrations usually go on for days, with music, singing, and fine foods.

## FESTIVAL CUSTOMS

Muslim festivals are serious religious occasions but they are also public holidays. For example, after the month of fasting for Ramadan, Muslims gather together for Eid al Fitr, a three-day celebration, when they dress up in new clothes, enjoy feasting, and give each other gifts.

The end of Ramadan is a great cause for celebration across the Islamic Empires.

### MIND YOUR MANNERS!

Table manners are considered very important in the Islamic Empires.

- At mealtimes, you must always wash your hands before sitting down on the floor on a rug or small pillow.
- When seated, never point the soles of your feet towards another person. This is a great insult because feet are considered dirty.
- There are no knives and forks — you will be expected to eat using your right hand only.
- When you meet someone new, you must also remember to shake with your right hand because it would be a great insult to use the left. People in the Islamic Empires use their left hand for washing. (There's no toilet paper in the Islamic Empires, so you have to use soap and water instead.)

The remarkable spiral minaret of the Great Mosque at Samarra is a must-see for sightseers visiting the Islamic Empires.

# CHAPTER 3

# SIGHTSEEING

There are some top attractions in the Islamic Empires that everyone should see. The palaces are decorated with gold and precious materials, and the mosques are places of great beauty and peace. And in the huge, newly built city of Baghdad you can visit zoos, museums, and gardens and try some of the most delicious food in the world. But make sure you visit at the right time, or you could find yourself dodging arrows and severed heads!

# BAGHDAD

For a weekend city break, Baghdad is definitely the place to go. Completed in AD 762, it took 100,000 architects, craftsmen, and workers from all over the Islamic world to build. But take care not to visit between AD 836 and 892. During this time the caliph moved his court to Samarra and warring rulers caused great trouble in the city. At one stage, rocks, severed heads from enemy warriors, and flaming pots of oil rained down on Baghdad, all shot from catapults outside the city gates!

Get your camera ready! Ancient Baghdad is bursting with beautiful buildings such as this 9th-century caliph's wife's tomb.

← 

## CIRCULAR CITY

You can get your bearings in Baghdad in a day because it was designed as two circles, one inside the other, with the outer one about 2 kilometres (1 mile) in diameter. Roads run outwards towards all parts of the Islamic world.

**THE SKY AT NIGHT**

Visit the Shammasiya **observatory** at night and see the caliph's astronomers at work. They have made wonderful maps of the stars and are busy calculating the length of a year.

Baghdad is a rich colourful place, with mosques and museums, zoos and libraries. Cooks here are famous for their elaborate dishes. Typical sweets include halvah (made from sesame seeds) and baklava (made from pastry, spices, and chopped nuts).

## A TOUR OF THE CITY

Follow these directions for an interesting tour of the city.

1. Start on the outskirts and follow the busy markets to the moat. Pass through one of the four gates in the double-brick outer city walls. The crowded streets inside are packed with small houses, where the poorer people live.

2. Towards the centre you should see a green dome with the figure of a rider holding a spear on top of the caliph's palace. The wider streets here are lined with shops and large merchants' houses. At the famous House of Wisdom you can see scholars discussing new ideas and inventions. Try asking them to turn lead coins into gold...

3. When you reach the second set of city walls it could take a while to get past the guards at the gate. They check visitors carefully, but it's worth the wait. Inside is the heart of the city, with the government buildings, grand mosque, and sumptuous royal palace.

**FROM LEAD TO GOLD**

Some Arabic scholars at this time believed that any metal could be changed into gold or silver if they could discover a rare substance, known as *al-iksir* (hence the English word elixir), a red powder made from a legendary "philosopher's stone".

# PALACES AND FORTRESSES

The other must-see buildings are the palaces. These huge constructions are designed to show off the power of the sultans, caliphs, princes, and amirs who live in them. They are often built like castles to keep out enemy forces.

A typical grand palace usually contains a maze-like sequence of rooms. These include a private mosque or place for prayer and separate living quarters for the owner, his family, his many wives, servants, advisers, and soldiers and their horses. The palace often has its own water and food stores so that people inside can remain self-sufficient during a siege.

## SHOWING OFF WEALTH

Rulers like to show off their wealth so they fill their palaces with rare items from the far corners of the Islamic world. Rooms are often lined with imported stone such as marble and jade, rare woods, and finely woven wall hangings. If you get a chance to go into a palace, don't be put off by the servants. They'll try to sprinkle you with rosewater so your smell doesn't offend the delicate royal noses!

Get away from the heat by wandering amongst the shady plants in the gardens. You'll also enjoy the soothing sound of the fountains, although your peace may be interrupted by strange noises. Many of the wealthiest rulers have zoos in their palaces, stocked with exotic animals, such as zebras, from across the empires.

### THE HALL OF THE TREE

At the sultan's palace in Baghdad ask if you can see the Hall of the Tree. This is a special room the caliph had made to keep him amused. It contains a huge artificial tree, made entirely of gold and silver and filled with gold mechanical birds that chirp.

# THE CITADEL OF ALEPPO

There are fortresses dotted all over the empires to make sure Islamic forces are not overthrown. There are lots to visit but one of the best is the Citadel of Aleppo in Syria. The only way in is over a narrow bridge across the wide moat and through a series of three iron doors. Beyond this is a dark twisting entrance passage with slit windows high above it. Glance up to check soldiers are not preparing to pour boiling oil on to you, mistaking you for an enemy!

You can't miss the enormous citadel in Aleppo, built high on a hill overlooking the flat lands all around.

# MOSTLY MOSQUES

Follow in the footsteps of Muhammad and visit some of the holiest places in the Islamic Empires, where the Prophet spent his life. Apart from the **Ka'bah** in Mecca, you should try to visit the mosque in nearby Madinah. Its shape is based on the Prophet's house, which was built around an open, square, walled courtyard. When it was first constructed, the mosque building had simple mud walls but successive empires redecorated it with marble and other expensive materials. The Prophet is buried under the stone floor.

## THE DOME OF THE ROCK

From Madinah, it is a long, hot journey to Jerusalem to see the Dome of the Rock. This is a beautiful octagonal building with a golden dome on top. Inside is a rock, but not just any rock. This is where Muslims believe Muhammad went up to Allah in Heaven. It was originally a Jewish temple because the rock is also important to Jews, who believe it symbolizes the foundation stone upon which the world was built.

### HOW ARE MOSQUES USED?

This checklist will help you work out what's what in a mosque.

Minaret: Most mosques have towers called minarets that the muezzin climbs to call in all directions.

Mihrab: A hollow in the wall that reminds worshippers which way Mecca is.

Minbar: A raised seat or platform with steps leading to it, from which the imam leads communal prayer or delivers a sermon.

Mosques are sacred buildings that have to be big enough to accommodate lots of worshippers. Mosques are also centres for the Islamic community. There are many separate rooms around the courtyards. Some rooms are used as madrassahs (religious schools) where people come to learn about the Qur'an. The courtyards themselves are often used for political and social purposes, such as concerts of religious music or recruitment of soldiers.

# THE GREAT MOSQUE AT CORDOBA

When the Abbasid Empire replaced the Umayyad Empire in AD 750, an Umayyad prince called Abd al-Rahman moved to Spain and created a new outpost of the Islamic world. Cordoba was its capital and the Great Mosque was its jewel. Plain on the outside, the interior is a vast hall with a roof supported high up by striped double arches resting on stone columns. The arched shapes look rather like the palm trees, the trunks of which supported the roof on Muhammad's home.

You'll feel small in the Great Mosque of Cordoba. It was built to be large enough for all Muslims in the city to meet in prayer.

# DECORATIVE DESIGNS

You will soon notice that many Islamic buildings, especially mosques and palaces, and also objects such as plates, books, and bowls, are decorated with writing. This beautiful writing is called **calligraphy**.

The best calligraphers in the Islamic Empires, such as the 11th-century master Ibn al-Bawwab, devote their lives to the art. They become so famous that they get to write just for the rich and powerful. Their tools are hand-cut reed pens, fine papers, and specially prepared inks. To decorate large surfaces on buildings, skilled masons carve calligraphy directly into stone or brick, and builders cement on tiles painted with words.

Here are some excellent places to spot beautiful calligraphy:
- around the top of the Dome of the Rock (see top right of picture opposite)
- on the Friday Mosque in Isfahan, Iran
- in the public libraries:
  see if you can find examples of calligraphy where the letters of a word are drawn in special shapes so they look like animals.

## I-SPY PATTERNS

On buildings throughout the Islamic Empires there are lots of geometric patterns to look out for. There are regular shapes, such as squares, rectangles, circles, pentagons, and triangles, that are repeated and linked together in interesting ways. In Islam these patterns represent the order and infinite power of Allah. Some shapes have special meanings. For example, stars represent the spreading of the Islamic world in all directions from the centre. They have 5, 6, 8, 10, 12, or even 16 points and are designed by dividing a circle into equal parts.

## IMAGE-FREE ZONE

You will not see pictures or models of people on mosques. This is rather different from European churches, where there are statues and paintings of saints. This tradition comes from the belief of many Muslims that, as Allah created people and animals, it is disrespectful for humans to try to recreate them. Other Muslims do think it is all right to make paintings of great rulers or military leaders, and life in the Islamic Empires. But these mostly appear as illustrations in non-religious books and are therefore small and very detailed.

Glazed tiles are used to add colour and make Islamic buildings weatherproof.

Beautiful rugs and carpets are on sale in many bazaars in the Islamic Empires.

# CHAPTER 4

# THINGS TO DO

There is plenty to keep you busy in the Islamic Empires besides sightseeing. You can borrow a horse and try to score a goal in a fast, furious polo game. If you are feeling brave (and strong) you could try your luck in a sweaty wrestling match. And after a tiring day's shopping and bargaining in the bustling bazaars there are many ways to relax. Pull up a cushion with the locals for a game of chess, listen to a talented musician, or marvel at a storyteller's accounts of great battles and faraway places.

# SPORTS AND GAMES

Young men in the Islamic Empires are encouraged to take part in sport to become strong and competitive. This will make them good business leaders and warriors. But, like many things in the Islamic Empires, what you get to do might depend on who you know. Caliphs, courtiers, and wealthy men do archery or go hunting with falcons, or go horse racing and play polo. Ordinary people don't have the time or money to do these things, but they might watch cock fights and ram fights.

## RACING AND POLO

Racing is probably the most popular sport – there's horse racing, boat racing, and even camel racing. The sleek Arabian horse is extremely fast. Horse racing is excellent for training cavalry officers because battles often take place between armies on horseback, with archers shooting as they ride. Polo is an Islamic invention and is also good for riding skills. It's a bit like hockey on horseback.

In polo, two teams of riders compete to knock a wooden ball into a goal, using a long wooden mallet.

## POLO RULES

The 9th-century Muslim writer Dinvari listed some rules for polo players, such as:
- Polo requires a great deal of exercise.
- If a polo stick breaks during a game it is a sign of inefficiency.
- A player should strictly avoid using strong language and should be patient.

# PLAYING CHESS

Chess is all the rage in the Islamic Empires. The Arabs learned to play chess from the Sassanids when they conquered them and took over the Persian Empire in AD 651. Like Chinese Whispers, the game of chess was passed on and on! The Persians probably learned it from the Indians, and the Indians themselves probably learned a version of it from the Chinese. After the Arabs took over Spain, chess gradually passed on to Europe too.

## WARNING!

Board games such as chess may not be as peaceful as they first appear – chess was encouraged because it was good for developing war strategy skills!
If you play chess against a caliph, make sure you lose. Caliphs enjoy playing chess so much that some are rumoured to have continued their game while battles raged outside their palace. But they are sore losers and people who beat them tend to be executed immediately!

# MUSIC AND STORYTELLING

Music and storytelling are very popular throughout the Islamic Empires. Some of the musical entertainment you will hear is religious. Praise-songs, which literally sing the praises of the Prophet Muhammad, began after his death and you will often hear Islamic chanting during Ramadan.

Caliphs pay musicians and dancers to entertain them at court, and female slaves are often trained to play music for the sultans. Favourite instruments include the lute, a four-stringed instrument called the oud, the tambourine-like riq, finger cymbals, drums made of clay with goatskin, and the ney (a long cane flute).

Several musicians can be seen here playing drums and other instruments at a royal wedding.

Across the Islamic Empires, many local folk music and dance traditions continued after the people became Muslims. For example, the **Bedouin** nomads still sing and dance the ancient songs of the desert. Some folk dances celebrate warriors' achievements, such as the Arabian sword dance; others celebrate the harvests or the changing seasons. You'll also see some folk singers busking on the streets.

## ENTERTAINMENT RULES

In many parts of the Islamic Empires dancing is allowed and enjoyed. But don't get carried away by the music and ask for a dancing partner. Men and women are not allowed to dance together.

## STORIES AND BOOKS

On the streets and in dining halls in some towns and cities, poets and storytellers entertain people with exotic tales full of excitement and romance. Thanks to Muslim scholars, you can also buy your own books. Muslims learned how to make paper from the Chinese papermakers. Paper soon replaced parchment (animal hides) and papyrus (made from reed plants) because it could be made virtually anywhere from rags and waste fibres.

Islamic libraries have hundreds of thousands of books, compared to the small libraries in **monasteries** and universities in the West at this time. There are more than 100 paper shops and bookshops in Papersellers' Street near the main mosque in Baghdad.

### ARABIAN NIGHTS

If you're looking for a book to keep you amused on your journey, pick up a copy of *The Arabian Nights*. This book tells the story of Scheherazade, a beautiful queen who tells her cruel new husband stories every night for 1,001 nights. She always finishes on a cliff-hanger so he won't kill her in the morning, as he had done to many wives before. Finally she cures him of his murderous habit. The book is full of colourful characters such as Aladdin, Sinbad, and Ali Baba and the 40 thieves.

# SHOPPING

If you like to shop until you drop, then you have come to the right place in the right time! The **bazaars** of the Islamic Empires are packed with lovely things to tempt you. But first make sure you have the right **currency**.

For large purchases you'll need dinars (coins made with gold brought from Africa). Smaller coins include the silver dirhem and the copper fals. Most are beautifully decorated with verses from the Qur'an. And if you leave your purse at home, some merchants will let you buy goods with an order of payment, which works like a modern cheque.

The coins of the Islamic Empires are marked with their name, the place they were made (or minted), and the year they were made.

## PRAYER MATS AND WOVEN GOODS

There is a great tradition of weaving rugs and blankets here. Nomads need rugs and cushions to sit on in their tents that are easy to pack up when they move from place to place. Prayer mats are designed for one person to kneel and pray on. There is often a colourful pattern pointing towards the top of the prayer mat so Muslims can place the rug facing towards Mecca when they pray.

### A BRAYING SHOPPING TROLLEY

There are so many souvenirs to choose from, you might end up buying rather a lot from Muslim bazaars. How will you get all your purchases home? Hire a donkey, as the locals do. In the Islamic Empires donkeys are "beasts of burden" and are used to carry heavy loads over short distances.

## JEWELLERY, POTTERY, AND PAINTINGS

The jewellery worn by the nomads makes a lovely gift. You can get earrings, necklaces, belts, ankle and hand decorations, and even nose-rings made out of silver in the Middle East. You can also pick up beautiful bronze, copper, brass, silver, and gold objects.

This little 10th-century deer from Cordoba would make an unusual ornament.

Some stalls offer pottery tiles, dishes, or pots often decorated with calligraphy, and swirling or geometric designs. The king and his family get all the best pieces but you should still find some good souvenirs. If you've got the time and money, why not have a miniature portrait painted? Miniature paintings are very fashionable. You could even have yourself drawn as part of a lavish court or heroic battle scene, as many of the rulers do.

The 13th-century Great Mosque of Divrigi, in Turkey, also served as a hospital and medical school.

# CHAPTER 5

# HEALTH AND SAFETY

Before you take a trip anywhere in this period, remember to get your innoculations (jabs) up to date. There are many fatal diseases around in the Islamic Empires that we no longer have to worry about today, such as smallpox. You should be safe most of the time, partly because caliphs keep roads safe for travellers so that Muslims can travel to Mecca freely. But this is also a violent time and you may find yourself in danger if you don't know the rules.

# HEALTH AND HYGIENE

There is no excuse for not keeping clean and smelling sweet while you are on holiday in the Islamic Empires. One of the Prophet's teachings is the importance of keeping your body clean. This makes the Islamic Empires cleaner and healthier than most other parts of the world at this time. Most houses have drains to take away dirty water, and every town has at least one if not several public bath houses (**hammams**). They are open from early in the morning until late at night. They are also cheap to visit so everyone can afford to bathe regularly.

## TIME FOR TEETH

If you forget to pack a toothbrush, use a miswak stick, and sweeten your breath with herbs and spices like the locals. Dentists here will pull out bad teeth and can also make you a false set, if you don't mind them being made out of bone!

Inside a public bath house. ↘

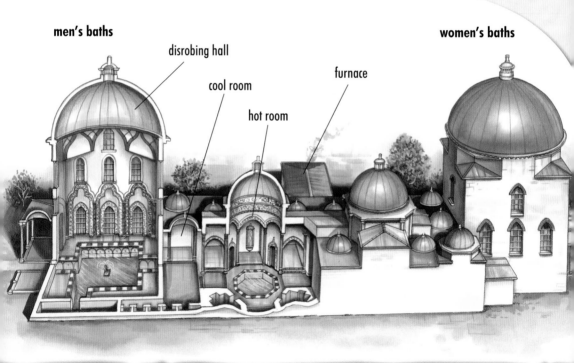

men's baths

disrobing hall

cool room

hot room

furnace

women's baths

# VISITING A HAMMAM

Here are a few things you need to know before you go.

- Hammams have separate sections for men and women, or men and women visit at separate times of day. Check this before you enter.
- In the women-only section you can strip off but the men are expected to wear towels around their waists.
- You are only allowed to visit the barber if you haven't eaten garlic, as this is considered very impolite and unfair on him!
- There are usually three rooms. The hot room generally has a large domed ceiling and a marble slab where you can get a massage. The warm room is for washing, and the cool room is where you go to relax and drink tea.

Hammams are not just places to wash. You can also catch up on local news and gossip, meet people, relax, drink tea, and even get a haircut and a massage.

## HYGIENE POLICE

In Islamic cities, the Muhtasib (public service inspectors) enforce strict hygiene regulations. They check restaurants, butchers, and slaughterhouses to see that the hygiene rules are being followed and anyone caught selling rotten meat is executed. They also check the quality of the water in hammams, and ensure that people obey the rules and don't dump their rubbish on the streets. At this time, few people in Europe even had access to clean drinking water, regular baths, or a sewage system!

# DOCTORS AND HOSPITALS

If, after all your attempts to keep clean and avoid illness, you do need to see a doctor, you've come to the right place. Muslim doctors are very advanced, and their invention of hospital wards has saved thousands of lives. If you get ill in some other parts of the world at this time, you could find yourself sharing a pus-covered, flea-infested bed with five other people (some of whom might already be dead)! In the Islamic Empires, you will be treated in proper hospitals by skilled practitioners who understand the importance of hygiene.

## HOSPITAL CARE

Sultans and caliphs have built fine hospitals across many parts of the Islamic world. These treat anyone for free and are open 7 days a week and 24 hours a day. They have separate blocks for men and women and separate wards for people with different diseases in order to limit the spread of disease. Each hospital has staff who specialize in different fields of medicine, from surgeons to bone-setters. And there is no need to worry if you get sick out of town – one of the latest mobile hospitals should come along soon. Medical teams on horseback, fully equipped with medicines and medical instruments, set up tents in remote villages to treat patients. They also follow armies into battle.

### DOCTORS AND DISEASE

Doctors in the Islamic Empires came up with the idea that disease was caused and spread by the tiny organisms we call germs today. If you happen to be in Baghdad in around AD 900 you'll see something very odd! This is when Doctor al-Razi famously chose the site for a new hospital in Baghdad by hanging pieces of meat in different parts of the city and examined them to see which took the longest time to go rotten. This made him the first doctor to link food decay with the quality of air in a place and to link that with the possible spread of infection.

## BLOODLETTING

In spite of many huge medical advances Muslim practitioners, like many doctors in Europe at this time, also use bloodletting (or "cupping") to draw inflammation to the surface of the body or to take away aches and pains. A cut is made in the skin (often on the patient's back) and a cup put over the area to create suction to pull out a small amount of blood. Yuck!

While patients in other countries have to bite down on a stick to endure the pain of an operation, Islamic doctors have invented anaesthetics that allow their patients to sleep through it! They give patients substances such as opium or lettuce seed to knock them out.

If you got sick 1,000 years ago, your best bet for survival was to get an appointment with one of the highly trained doctors of the Islamic Empires.

# KEEPING SAFE

Even though wars are common and life can be pretty violent, the age of the Islamic Empires is a safer time to travel than ever before. Before Islam, nomadic tribes would frequently rob and kill travellers. Muhammad and later Islamic leaders introduced laws to bring order to the empires. The caliph's officials would enforce some pretty stern punishments if these laws were disobeyed.

Here is a list of some typical punishments for law-breakers that you might see being carried out on the streets.
- Adultery: death by stoning
- Highway robbery: execution, or right hand and left foot cut off
- Theft: right hand cut off (second offence: left foot cut off)
- Drinking alcohol: 80 lashes with a whip

## DANGEROUS WORDS

Remember to mind your language. A slip of the tongue will be harshly punished. If a caliph objects to something you say, a simple wave of his hand can tell the executioner to put you to death immediately. And be careful what you write in letters home while on holiday. The caliphs have networks of spies to make sure everyone in the empires live by their rules. Ibn Muqla was an important calligrapher who had his right hand cut off for writing something rude about a caliph.

### THE EVIL EYE

If you still don't feel safe, invest in a charm to ward off evil. Many Muslims at this time, especially in North Africa, believe that certain people can spread bad luck through their eyes. To prevent the evil eye, you can buy magical objects such as "the hand of Fatimah" or raise your left hand in protection. So remember not to hold up your left hand as a greeting or people might take offence.

Here a vizier (official of the Muslim court), watches as a criminal is executed.

# DHIMMIES

If you are not a Muslim, one way of ensuring safe passage through the Islamic Empires is to become a dhimmie. Dhimmies are people who do not want to become Muslims but want to be part of the Islamic Empires, so they pay a tax to the ruler. By doing so they become dhimmies, which means "protected people". In this way, they gain the same rights as Muslims and the protection of the Islamic government.

**HEADS OFF!**

If you want to keep your head, never say anything that might be understood as blasphemous (an insult to Allah or Islam). This is the worst sin you could commit in the Islamic Empires and it is punishable by death.

Decorative mosaics adorn a wall inside the Friday Mosque in Iran. The building is now a museum that houses examples of Islamic architecture dating back to the 11th century.

# CHAPTER 6

# USEFUL INFORMATION

This is an easy reference guide for the time traveller visiting the Islamic Empires. First there is a phrase book to help you read the beautiful Arabic script, and a numbers guide to help you understand how much everything is going to cost you. There's also a brief history section to explain what brought about the end of the Golden Age of the Islamic Empires and to warn you about some of the bloody battles that caused its downfall. Finally, there is a timeline so you can check at a glance what times you need to visit in order to see particular events or people.

| | |
|---|---|
| A | ﺍ |
| B | ﺏ |
| T | ﺕ |
| TH | ﺙ |
| J | ﺝ |
| H | ﺡ |
| KH | ﺥ |
| D | ﺩ |
| Z or DH | ﺫ |
| R | ﺭ |
| Z | ﺯ |
| S | ﺱ |
| SH | ﺵ |
| S | ﺹ |
| D | ﺽ |
| T | ﻁ |
| DH or Z | ﻅ |
| ' or 3 | ﻉ |
| GH | ﻍ |
| F | ﻑ |
| Q | ﻕ |
| K | ﻙ |
| L | ﻝ |
| M | ﻡ |
| N | ﻥ |
| H | ﻩ |
| W or U | ﻭ |
| Y or i | ﻱ |

# GETTING TO KNOW ARABIC

The Arabic language started as a dialect used by nomads in the Arabian deserts. The spread of the words of the Qur'an took Arabic across the Islamic world. Caliphs and other rulers and their administrators encouraged the use of one written form of the language so they could control their empires. With a little Arabic, everyone can understand each other, even though they might also speak other languages. Why not try learning a bit of Arabic yourself?

## USEFUL PHRASES

Here are some useful words and phrases, written as you say them in Arabic (not in Arabic symbols).

| English | Arabic pronunciation |
|---|---|
| Peace be upon you | As-salaamu 'aleykum |
| And upon you be peace... | Wa 'aleykum as-salaam |
| My name is... | Ana ismi... |
| What is your name? | Matha ismuka... |
| I want to buy... | Ana ureed an ashtiree... |
| I want to visit | Ana ureed an azoor... |
| I speak English | Ana Atakallum al-Injileeziya |
| How much? | Bikam? |
| That's expensive | Hatha ghaalee |
| Until we meet again | ila al-Liqa' |

✓ The Arabic alphabet has 28 symbols representing sounds and words. The symbols are written and read from right to left.

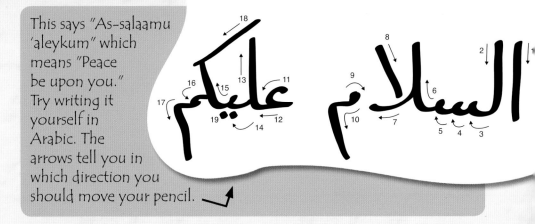

This says "As-salaamu 'aleykum" which means "Peace be upon you." Try writing it yourself in Arabic. The arrows tell you in which direction you should move your pencil.

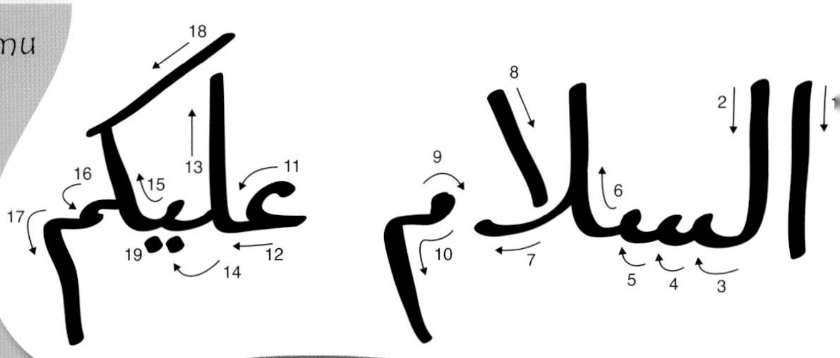
السلام عليكم
1
2
3
4
5
6
7
8
9
10
11
12
13
14
15
16
17
18
19

## STANDARD NUMBERS

At the start of the Islamic Empires people worked out sums in many different ways. Many merchants and traders counted on their fingers and wrote numbers in words. Others used letters of the alphabet to mean numbers. Using letters of the alphabet, the first nine letters represent 1 to 9, the next nine letters represent 10 to 90, the next nine 100–900, and z, the last letter, is 1,000. However, in the 8th century travellers brought back a newer system of writing numbers 1 to 9 using symbols from India. The symbols changed slightly as people accepted the system and learned to write them. This wasn't easy because, unlike letters, the numbers are written from left to right.

Eventually a standard form of Arabic numbers was used not only throughout the Islamic Empires, but also in Europe and other parts of the world. This was very important because it made international trade much easier.

You'll definitely recognize most of the numbers but beware: depending on when you go, 2 and 3 might be on their sides and 4 and 5 are most unusual.

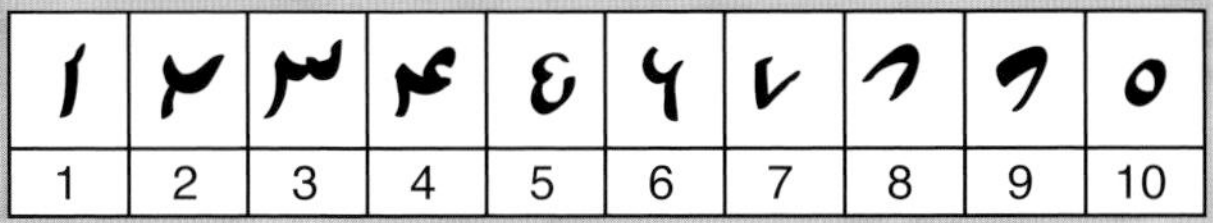
1
2
3
4
5
6
7
8
9
10

from 11th century

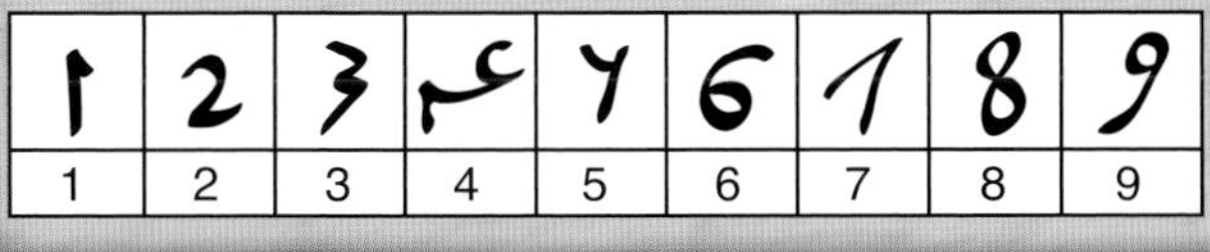
1
2
3
4
5
6
7
8
9

from 14th century

# END OF THE GOLDEN AGE

What should you expect to see if you arrive in the regions of the Islamic Empires after the end of its so-called Golden Age? The Abbasid caliphs are the last rulers of the Golden Age. By the 12th century their rule is becoming weaker as bickering over religious differences worsens and some rulers are assassinated.

## THE CRUSADES

The Islamic Empires are further weakened by the Crusades. These military campaigns from AD 1095 to 1291 were also known as holy wars. They were fought by Christian knights wanting to take the holy city of Jerusalem back from the Muslims and to help the Christian emperor of Constantinople in his wars against Muslim Turks. The battles continued for 200 years as Christians tried to get rid of Muslims from a far wider area, including Spain. By 1100 the Crusaders had claimed Jerusalem and it was ruled by a Christian king. But in 1187 Islamic leader and Egyptian sultan Salah al-Din won back the city. However, by 1291 many Muslim strongholds had fallen to the Christians and the Islamic military forces were badly weakened.

## MONGOL ATTACK

The final straw comes in 1258 when Baghdad is attacked and destroyed by the Mongols. This was the first time the Muslim world was overrun by non-Muslims. The Mongols left a trail of death and destruction from which the Abbasid Empire never recovered. Trade routes became unsafe and law and order broke down. The Golden Age had ended.

### BATTLE SCENES

If you have a strong stomach you could drop in on one of the battles during the Crusades. These were bloody affairs and at one point the streets of Jerusalem were said to be ankle-deep with blood. Weapons used included siege machines that battered down gates, bows and arrows, spears and swords, flame-throwers, and even exploding grenades.

# LATER EMPIRES

If you want to see the Islamic Empires after the Golden Age there are still some fascinating places to visit. For example, the Mongol emperor who conquered Baghdad converted to Islam, and ancestors of his who conquered India went on to rule the great Mughal Empire from 1526 until 1857. The Muslim Safavid Empire that ruled Iran from 1501 until 1736 is also worth a visit, especially if you stop over to see their elegant capital Isfahan. And the Ottomans, a dynasty of Turkish sultans who ruled much of the Mediterranean and the Middle East from the 14th century to the early 20th century, are known for their strict rule, sumptuous clothing, and beautiful tiled palaces and mosques.

## THE FALL OF BAGHDAD

If you do risk travelling to see the fall of Baghdad you'll be horrified by the change in the city. Two million Muslims are killed in the attack, and many mosques, hospitals, schools, and even roads and waterways are destroyed. So many books from the House of Wisdom are dumped in the Euphrates River that their ink turns its waters black.

Built in 1617, the Blue Mosque in Turkey has 260 windows that keep it well lit in daytime.

# THE ISLAMIC EMPIRES AT A GLANCE

## TIMELINE

| | |
|---|---|
| **AD 570** | Birth of Muhammad. |
| **610** | Muhammad receives first messages from the Angel Jibril (Gabriel). |
| **622** | The **hijrah** (when Muhammad and his followers were forced out of Mecca and moved to Madinah). |
| **632** | Death of Muhammad. Abu Bakr becomes the first caliph. |
| **634** | Abu Bakr dies and Umar becomes caliph. |
| **634–644** | Muslim armies invade Syria, Egypt, and Iraq. |
| **638** | Muslim soldiers take Jerusalem. |
| **644** | Umar is assassinated and Uthman becomes caliph. |
| **644–650** | Muslim armies invade Iran and Afghanistan and enter North Africa. |
| **656** | Uthman is assassinated and Ali becomes caliph. |
| **661** | Ali is assassinated and new caliph Muawiya is the first ruler of the Umayyad dynasty. |
| **685** | In Jerusalem work starts on the building of the Dome of the Rock. |
| **705** | The Great Mosque in Damascus is built. |
| **750** | The Abbasids take over from the Umayyads as rulers of the Islamic Empires. |
| **762** | Baghdad becomes capital of the Islamic Empires. |
| **784** | Work starts on the great Mosque of Cordoba, in Spain. |
| **836** | Capital of Islamic Empires moves to Samarra. |
| **892** | Capital of Islamic Empires moves back to Baghdad. |
| **969** | Fatimids defeat Abbasids in Egypt. |
| **973** | Fatimid rulers make Cairo, in Egypt, the Islamic Empires' capital. |

| 1206 | Mongol tribes unite under new leader Chinghis (Genghis) Khan. |
| 1258 | Mongols attack Baghdad, and Abbasid rule over the Islamic Empires comes to an end. |
| 1380s–1405 | Mongol leader Timur conquers much of central Asia, Iran, and Iraq. |
| 1453 | Ottomans capture Constantinople, in what is now Turkey, and rename it Istanbul. |
| 1492 | Christians achieve complete control of Spain. |
| 1501 | The Safavids found their empire in Iran. |
| 1520–1566 | The period of rule by Ottoman sultan Suleiman the Magnificent. |
| 1556–1605 | The period of rule of the first Mughal emperor in India, Akbar the Great. |
| 1628–1658 | Rule of famous Mughal emperor Shah Jahan who built the Taj Mahal. |

# FURTHER READING

## BOOKS

*Great Empires of the Past: Empire of the Islamic World*, Robin Doak (Facts on File, 2004)

*History in Art: Islamic Empires*, Nicola Barber (Raintree, 2005)

*World History: The Islamic Empire*, Phyllis Corzine (Lucent Books, 2004)

## WEBSITES

- http://www.pbs.org/empires/islam
  Click on "Educational resources" for many interesting articles about faith and culture in the Islamic Empires.

- http://www.historyforkids.org/learn/islam/history

- http://www.bbc.co.uk/religion/religions/islam/history

# GLOSSARY

**Abbasid** dynasty of caliphs and other leaders who ruled the second Islamic Empire from 750 to 1258

**Allah** Arabic word for God

**amir** military leader

**astrolabe** instrument used by sailors to read the positions of the stars and planets when navigating

**bazaar** open-air market with shops and stalls selling goods

**Bedouin** tribe of nomadic desert people from the Middle East and North Africa

**caliph** civil and religious ruler of a Muslim state or empire

**calligraphy** art of beautiful writing, especially in religious works

**caravan** long line of camels that travel across the Islamic Empires

**caravanserai** roadside inn where travellers can rest

**convert** someone who changes religion

**crusade** holy war

**currency** money or unit of exchange for goods or services

**dhow** ship with large triangular sails, used for trading

**dowry** gift of money or valuables made by a bride's family to a groom's family when the couple get married

**Fatimid** dynasty of caliphs and other leaders who ruled an Islamic Empire based in Cairo from 909 to 1171

**halal** Islamic religious food preparation laws

**hammam** public bath house

**harem** women's quarters in a Muslim palace or home

**hijrah** Muhammad's emigration with his followers from Mecca to Madinah in 622

**imam** person who leads prayers in mosque

**irrigate** water crops in fields

**Islam** religion based on the word of Allah, received by the Prophet Muhammad, and on Muhammad's teachings

**Ka'bah** square building in Mecca believed by Muslims to be the house Ibrahim erected for God and the focus of Muslim worship

**Madinah** city in Saudi Arabia where Muhammad lived after he became Prophet; also known as Medina

**madrassah** religious school linked to a mosque

**Mecca** holiest Muslim city

**monastery** place where a strict religious community lives

**Mongols** tribe of nomadic people from Mongolia, central Asia

**monsoon** season of very wet weather caused by moist winds blowing on to Asia from the Indian Ocean

**mosque** place of Muslim worship

**muezzin** man who calls Muslim worshippers to prayer

**Muhammad** founder of Islam, also known as the Prophet of God

**Muslim** person who believes in Islam

**nomad** member of ethnic group with no permanent homes, who moves animals between grazing places

**oasis** small area in the desert watered by springs and wells

**observatory** building from which people can study the stars

**pilgrimage** journey to a sacred place or shrine

**prophet** someone who hears and passes on the word of God

**Qur'an** sacred book of Islam

**Ramadan** month of fasting during hours of daylight

**revelations** God's word as passed to people

**Shahadah** the first pillar of Islam, the statement "There is no god but Allah, and Muhammad is his prophet."

**sheikh** Arab chief or prince

**sultan** king in the Islamic Empires

**Umayyad** dynasty of caliphs and other leaders who ruled the first Islamic Empire from 661 to 750

# INDEX